The Pro-Active Paraeducator: More than 250 Smart Ideas for Paraprofessionals who Support Teachers

Betty Y. Ashbaker

Brigham Young University

Provo, Utah, USA

Jill Morgan

Swansea Metropolitan University

Swansea, Wales, UK

ACKNOWLEDGEMENTS

We acknowledge the many generous and insightful contributions made over the years by dedicated teachers and paraeducators, as they have shared their experience and ingenuity with us.

Table of Contents

INTRODUCTION

This book will help you in your work as a paraeducator: the work of helping students to achieve success. Your job title may be *teacher's assistant, paraeducator, instructional assistant,* or *aide,* and your job description may cover instruction, clerical duties, supervision of students, or housekeeping tasks, but we use the word *paraeducator* as a general term to indicate that you work under the supervision of a professional educator. You may work under the close supervision of a teacher in a general classroom or one-to-one in a separate room with a single student; you may be a job coach, accompanying a student off-campus to work placement. Your work may be clearly defined for you, or you may have to make many instructional decisions on your own initiative. You may work with special education students or in a regular classroom, in the Title I program or in a computer lab.

Whatever your situation, you can gain more control of what happens: you can be a Proactive Paraeducator.

Paraeducator

Para: alongside

Educator: Supporting teaching and student learning

For those of you who work closely supervised, or whose work is very clearly defined, many decisions have already been made for you—usually by a teacher or immediate supervisor. However, there are many aspects of your work, which require your initiative and these decisions can be made beforehand. They should not be made on the spur of the moment merely as a reaction to student behaviors, and this is especially true if you work with groups of students. You need to decide how you will present material, decide what questions you will ask to monitor student under- standing, how you will supervise the students assigned to you, what incentives you can offer for good work, and how you want students to indicate that they want to contribute to a class discussion or answer a question. Be sure to check with your supervisor before implementing any of these practices, as it is a legal requirement to work under the direction of a professional. Nevertheless strategies and practices can be planned carefully in advance in a proactive manner. If a student acts inappropriately, you also need to be prepared with a reasonable response. That will be particularly difficult to do if you have not pre-planned your course of action.

Being a proactive paraeducator does not mean that you work contrary to the teacher's classroom rules or try to take inappropriate control. It means planning, asking yourself, "What would I do if..." and therefore being prepared. This proactive approach will help to prevent difficulties as students see your competence and know your expectations. It also helps them to know that their success is your first concern.

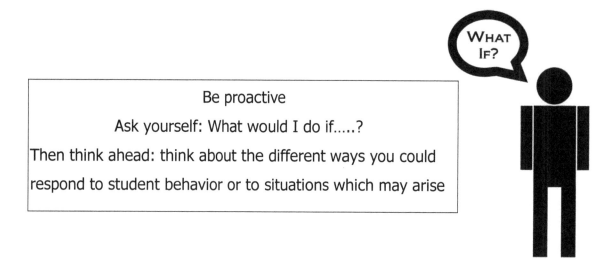

Be proactive

Ask yourself: What would I do if.....?

Then think ahead: think about the different ways you could respond to student behavior or to situations which may arise

This book contains many practical suggestions to help you in your everyday work. Many suggestions have been made by paraeducators like you, who have learned from experience the things that work best in their particular situation. There are also suggestions from teachers. And of course we draw on our own experience of schools and classrooms. Our aim is to give you a whole range of ideas and suggestions that you can apply to your work.

Some of the ideas may not be new to you, but simply need a review. This may just be a timely reminder of things that have worked well in the past, but that you have not used recently. And as you come across new ideas and useful suggestions through watching your supervising teacher or other teachers, attending training sessions, or talking to other paraeducators, you can add them at the end of the appropriate chapter.

The areas covered in this book include the following:

Promoting positive behavior: how to take a proactive approach to establishing rules for student behavior, and for your own roles and responsibilities; developing positive relationships with students, and other adults; and organizing for success.

Maximizing Use of Time: Making the best use of the time available to you and your students; and how to prevent disruptions so you can maximize learning opportunities.

Effective instructional strategies: This includes the basic steps of presenting and reviewing material, monitoring student understanding, and getting and giving feedback. There are many useful suggestions for how to get both group and individual feedback, and how to best respond to students, so that they feel confident and respected.

Being part of the instructional team: this chapter considers aspects of professionalism, and how you can work effectively to support the classroom team – a team which includes both adults and students – in the teaching and learning process.

Good, and getting better

An important aspect of being proactive is to make frequent self-assessments, and identify areas of personal strength, as well as areas in which you feel you could improve your work. Improvement can take time, and you can do this at your own pace, choosing any area of your work that you personally feel is important. However, two things are essential for your success:

1. The area you choose does *not* have to be the one in which you feel you are *least* competent. Working to enhance any skill is a positive, proactive step, so you can boost your motivation by choosing any area for improvement that will give you particular satisfaction; and

2. Set yourself a goal for change that is small and realistic. Becoming the perfect paraeducator overnight may be what you dream of, but in reality you know that change and improvement are only possible a very small step at a time. There are also many facets to perfecting your knowledge and skills, and you can't tackle them all at the same time. Being proactive and setting realistic goals will help prevent discouragement.

So when you have identified an area, such as, *monitoring student understanding,* you can choose one of the suggestions in this book, for example, "Ask as many questions as possible - it gives more students a chance to respond", and then set yourself a goal and a time for accomplishing it, and decide how you will check your progress. The last thing to do is to record your observations - What happened when you tried out the suggestion? Did it work? Did the students like it? What might you do differently next time to make it work better? This will help you set your next area of focus for change and improvement.

Did it work?

Did the students like it?

What could I do differently next time?

You will find a blank form for this process of goal setting and recording progress at the end of each chapter of the book, and an example has been filled out for you to follow on the next page. You can make as many more copies of the form as you need to make regular assessments of your own progress and identify areas in which you would like to see change and improvement.

The book is designed as a buffet, for dipping in and sampling – it isn't a set menu that has to be consumed in linear fashion from start to finish, one course or chapter at a time.

This book is also designed for paraeducators who work with a range of age groups and with students of varying abilities. Use your professional judgment to decide which of the suggestions best apply to your students, but don't automatically dismiss some of the suggestions which may appear to be for younger students if you only work in secondary school.

Older students do sometimes like to indulge in activities they have—perhaps with some regret—had to leave behind once they have left the elementary school. And of course some of the most able younger students will be able to engage in activities that you would generally associate with secondary school.

Setting goals for improvement in my work *(example)*

The area I'm going to focus on:

___*Monitoring Student Understanding*_____

The suggestion I'm going to use is:

__*Ask as many questions as possible - it gives more students a chance to respond*___

Time in which I'm going to try this suggestion:

_____*This coming week*_____

How will I check on my progress?

I'll try to write down a list of as many questions as I can think of to ask the students before each of my spelling groups. If I keep those in a folder, I can add to them each day, so at the end of the week I should have quite a good list.

What I noticed when I used the suggestion:

I felt like I was just firing one question after another at my students the first couple of groups, but I got used to it, and the students seemed to like having lots of opportunities to show what they knew. I think I'll have to get more stickers, though - or change the reward system – I'll have used up my supply by the end of next week!

How will I include my supervisor in this goal-setting process?

I'll ask my supervisor if I can observe her as she teaches, so that I can see how she gives more students a chance to respond.

Considerations in Protocol

There are many things that you must know as a paraeducator. However, some of these will not have a direct effect on how you function in the classroom or in your instructional role. But lack of knowledge and a mis-step could cost you your job! It would certainly impact negatively on your working relationships. You can be proactive in finding out some of the procedural requirements and expectations which others have of you. We have provided a checklist to help you avoid potential difficulties with your supervisor and administrator. Check off those items which you feel comfortable with, and take action on those which you are unsure of.

? What is the procedure for obtaining the supplies I need (paper, markers, etc.) for my work with students?

? What are the procedures I must follow if I purchase supplies and need to be reimbursed?

? What is the school policy and my teacher's preference for using my cell phone (or other personal technology) in the classroom?

? What do I do if a parent asks me for information about a student's progress, or a teacher's effectiveness?

? Does it make any difference whether the parent asks me for information when I am at home, at church, at civic league, or at the store?

? Who do I talk to if I have a complaint to make? Is there a form to fill out? What if my complaint is about my teacher?

? What do I do if there are policies or procedures that I don't agree with? Who do I go to?

CHAPTER 1: PROMOTING POSITIVE BEHAVIOR

This chapter is dedicated to promoting positive behavior: how to support an atmosphere conducive to student learning with the minimum number of distractions from such things as student misbehavior, misunderstandings, or a lack of trust and respect between those who work in the classroom. As was stated before, whatever the situation you work in, you can take responsibility for the time, the space and the students that are assigned to you. Being a proactive paraeducator means planning ahead to prevent difficulties, and devoting your energies to supporting a positive environment. This chapter will cover three important areas:

1. Establishing positive relationships - with students and with your supervisor;
2. Knowing and supporting the rules for students behavior; and
3. Organizing for the success of everyone in the classroom.

We begin with suggestions for establishing positive relationships with students, as this is an aspect of your work which is universally important. Then we move on to discussing rules – which help to strengthen relationships with students, and also give a clear focus for your work together.

How does this apply to you?

Consider your assignment. If you are in the classroom most of the day with your teacher, many classroom management decisions have already been made for you, and as you work under the teacher's supervision this is appropriate. However, you may be taking students out of the classroom, or away from the larger group to a corner of the room. In this case, it is important that you establish rules and procedures for your working area and teach them to the students. Consider all of the suggestions in this chapter in the light of your assignment, but check with your supervising teacher if you wish to make major procedural changes.

Establishing positive relationships with students

This section about establishing positive relationships with students is not a section about how to make friends with students or how to 'get them on your side.' It's about being proactive in attending to the aspects of your work which will make a real difference. And as you work in a context which is likely to be full of people – mostly students – the interpersonal relationships you develop are crucial to your success in supporting student learning.

√ Consider your students' best interests when you seek to establish a relationship with them. It may be nice to be popular, but it may not help students to achieve. So you may sometimes have to be less of a friend and more of a teacher.

√ "Flowers grow out of dark moments" so always look for the flowers (successes/positives). Take time each day if you can – perhaps while you are going home from work – to reflect on the day's successes and acknowledge the positive contributions you have been able to make to student achievement, and the positive interactions you have had with students. Even the worst days at work have some positive moments.

√ Be honest in your interactions with your students. Explain your actions when it is appropriate.

√ Remember to practice what you preach and keep your social skills polished so that you are poised during interactions with students and the adults you work with.

√ If you keep focused on a student you are working with, and refuse to be distracted or interrupted by other students and their requests, you send a powerful message to that student. You are saying s/he is the most important person at that moment, and that you are there to meet his/her needs.

√ Can you remember how much "work" it took to learn some of the things you know? Remind yourself of this when students struggle, and help them to work through their difficulties.

√ Be aware of what students accomplish outside of class (student leadership, athletics, 4-H, scouting, etc) and recognize their accomplishments when you can.

√ Have extra chairs placed around the room so that you can sit down as you circulate to help students rather than always standing over them. It is less intimidating - and it's easier on your back!

√ If a student is hesitant to respond, help him/her to figure out the answer rather than calling on another student. This will help the student to gain confidence, it shows your belief in his/her ability, and it demonstrates to other students that it is important to think things through - that finding the right answer is more important than speed.

√ Let students know if there is a reinforcing activity that is contingent on completing a particular task. For example, at the beginning of the activity tell students, "When you finish this math sheet, it will be time for recess," or "If you complete this assignment quickly and accurately, you'll have time to work on your other projects." The reinforcing activity should be something truly reinforcing for the student – something that will motivate them – and should therefore sometimes include a free choice of activity or something meaningful to the student's learning, but that feels less like 'more work'.

√ Train students to say "I don't know" rather than not responding. Likewise, teach students that it is not appropriate to laugh at or mock someone who says. "I don't know." Let them know it is smart to admit that they don't know, because then you can help them in whatever way they need. In fact if they don't admit to not knowing, you may not even know that they need help.

√ Try to provide students with positive learning activities that link material presented in class with their everyday lives. This makes education much more relevant for them.

√ Help students remember assignments by writing them on the whiteboard rather than only presenting them orally. It will be especially helpful for those students who do not easily recall spoken instructions and need the written prompt. If you leave the assignment list in the student's individual folder or desk, it will also act as a reminder.

Feedback

√ Use correction instead of criticism. For example, "Sit in your assigned seat, please" rather than "You're always creating problems by sitting in someone else's chair". It serves as a good reminder of the behavior that is expected.

√ When you correct a student's work, try to focus on the assignment rather than the student. Then if something is incorrect, the focus is on the answer being wrong, rather than the student. Make sure you clearly explain how the answer relates directly to the requirement of the assignment rather than the efforts of the student. You'll find an example of this in the nearby box.

√ You may be sincere in the things you say to students and other adults you work with, but it's difficult to sound sincere if you use the same phrases every time. Make a list of ways of showing your appreciation. Here are some to start you off.

Good job working so fast!   That answer was really helpful.

I'd never thought of that idea.   That's really useful suggestion.

√ Even if the praise you give is sincere, it needs to be linked to the action you are praising in order to make it really effective.

Ethan has just completed the task assigned to the class – drawing a map to show the layout of the school. However, he hasn't followed the instructions the teacher gave him, and you know that he was passing notes to his friend while the teacher was giving those instructions. You have two choices:

1. point out to Ethan that it's no surprise that he completed his assignment all wrong because he wasn't paying attention when the teacher gave out the instructions, so he'll have to start over; or

2. focus on the aspects of the assignment that are correct – there's always something positive you can recognize, and after all he has completed the task – and then prompt him to add or edit his work, to make improvements, and so that it conforms more closely with what the teacher expects.

Ethan is much more likely to be willing to hear your suggestions for improvement if you have acknowledged positive aspects of his behavior and work first. Recriminations only serve to antagonize students.

Fairness

√ Honestly consider your attitudes and analyze your practice in regard to gender, as any bias of this kind is likely to have a negative effect on some of your students. Do you expect boys to do better in math and science, and therefore do you give them more opportunities in these subjects than girls? And do you expect girls to do better in subjects like home economics (or to know more about social science subjects), and therefore never ask questions of boys when these subjects occur?

Deliberately set aside time to record the questions you ask, and who you ask for responses. Draw a line down the center of a piece of paper, with B for boys at the top of one side and G for girls at the top of the other. Make a tally in the proper column each time you call on a student during a particular lesson, then count them up. How did you do? Did you favor the boys more than the girls? Or vice versa? Once you have established whether you give more opportunities for responding to boys or girls, take the further step of considering the level of difficulty of the responses you expect from boys rather than girls.

√ Try to divide your time and attention among all of your students - remember that those who are behaving and those who are coping well with their work deserve your time and attention just as much as those who are experiencing difficulties. Students shouldn't be "rewarded" by your attention only if they behave badly or struggle with their work. Although you don't want to keep interrupting capable students who are on-task by asking if they need anything, or even offering praise, you can support them by taking time to extend their thinking when they have completed an assignment.

√ If you feel that you are justified in extending a deadline for an assignment because of difficulties which one student is experiencing, then give the whole class the same option, not just the one student (but check with the teacher first before you change arrangements he or she has made).

√ Try to have some positive personal contact with every student every day. It may be difficult to find time to talk to your supervising teacher each day – particularly if you work in a different physical space - but try to have some personal contact there too!

√ Take an interest in what your students do outside of the classroom and have them share their interests with each other. Students could write something they do in their spare time on a piece of paper, put the papers in a jar, and pull them out one at a time to guess which student matches which activity. This gives students more opportunities to connect with each other, and with you, as you all get to know each other better.

√ To show appreciation for uniqueness, you can play a game with counters (e.g. buttons, poker chips or other tokens). Everyone starts off with the same number of counters as there are people in the group (this is easier with groups of 15 or less, but it can be done with more). Then each person, in turn, makes a statement about his or her self that is unique (e.g. she's one of twins, or he's been to Australia, or he has no cousins). Anyone in the group who <u>can't</u> say that about himself has to give a counter to the person who just made the statement. Those who <u>can</u> say the same thing about themselves don't have to give up a counter. And so it goes on, with everyone having a turn (or more turns if you wish, and have a small enough group), and the counters being added up at the end. The 'winner' is the person with most counters. That is, they are the person who has the most unique points. You can decide whether the student in question is likely to be comfortable having you highlight their uniqueness, or whether you engage in the activity as an interesting way of getting to know each other better, without announcing a 'winner'.

√ If something is not done the way you expected, before you question the person involved, ask yourself: Did I give clear directions? or Did I misunderstand what was to be done?

Supporting rules for student behavior

Rules are guidelines that define what constitutes acceptable and unacceptable behavior. In sports there are rules for such things as how many players are in a team, what a team has to do to score points or goals, and what it means to be 'off- side' or why a team might be awarded penalty points. Students are often quite knowledgeable about rules for different sports and may play on sports teams themselves. School rules are essentially no different: they should clearly define what constitutes acceptable and unacceptable behavior; they should also clearly outline the rewards a student can expect for behaving in an acceptable manner, as well as the penalties they may incur if they behave in an unacceptable manner. In the same way that sports rules allow a number of participants to enjoy playing together in a purposeful way that is commonly understood, school and class rules allow students and adults to enjoy interacting while engaging in the activities associated with teaching and learning.

√ Being proactive in the classroom means thinking "What do I do if...?" and considering beforehand what you would do in a particular situation. What if a student disobeys a rule? What if you don't agree with what your supervising teacher asks you to do? What if one of your students is too shy to offer a response in class? What will you do in these situations? You won't be able to prepare for every eventuality because students are particularly good at surprising us with their behavior, but you can mentally and physically prepare for many typical classroom situations. Make a list of the rules for the class or setting where you work, and write some 'What if's....' for each of the rules, along with how you would respond to that type of situation.

School rules

√ Rules of conduct for the entire school are out of your control to change, but it is appropriate to remind students what they are, and how they apply to the classroom as well as the rest of the school. You can also emphasize the benefits of school rules for the students themselves.

√ Remember that if you work with more than one teacher, different classrooms may have somewhat different rules. For example, in one classroom students may get a drink without asking permission, while in another classroom they may require the teacher's permission. Be sure that you know which rules apply in each class so that you can give consistent support to each teacher.

Setting Clear Expectations

√ Whenever possible, state rules in positive terms rather than a list of "Don'ts" (e.g. "Walk quietly to your next activity" rather than, "Don't run!.")

Examples of rules expressed in positive ways

Walk in the hallways

Respect other people's space and property

One person talking at a time

√ Let students know what you *do* want them to do, not just what you *don't* want them to do. It gives them a range of options for positive, acceptable behavior rather than just a list of restrictions. They may also be able to suggest other behaviors they think are acceptable and you can confirm for them whether those behaviors are acceptable or not.

√ When you describe appropriate behavior to students, be explicit and speak to your students' level of understanding. For example, the rule "We work together and help each other" might refer to sharing toys for a kindergartner, but for an 8th grader it would more likely involve collaborating with other students on a research project.

√ Be clear about which classroom rules apply when students are working with you in a small group and which do not. Do they need to raise a hand to respond if there are only 3 of them? Do they still need to observe the rule of courtesy to each other? Discuss why some rules may change but others remain the same whatever the work group.

√ Classrooms can receive new students throughout the school year so you may need to review rules, especially after vacation breaks or when new students join the class.

Including students

√ If students can have a sense of ownership in rules and understand the reasons for them, they are more likely to follow them. Discuss the rules with students and ask them to relate why the rules are appropriate and reasonable.

√ Plan when and how you will discuss rules and procedures, and model or have students practice the procedures. Use the "What if... game." You might ask students: "We have the rule that says you must stay in your seat, but what if... James needed to sharpen his pencil?" Have students discuss whether the rule still applies in that situation, then have them provide "What if...'s?" themselves so that you can help them understand the extent of the rule.

√ Keeping students busy and productive is the best and most effective way of reducing disruptive behavior, and therefore helping them to keep to the school and class rules.

√ Check the extent to which you include all students in activities, whatever their gender, ethnic background or abilities.

√ *Diversity* generally refers to students being from different backgrounds. Although language is the most obvious form of diversity, it can also refer to differences in family structure, religion, values and race. Use the diversity of your students as a resource, and learn to see it as a strength.

√ Accommodate students' varying learning styles and preferences by thinking of ways you can help them be comfortable in the learning environment.

√ All students need to feel valued and included and that they are in a safe environment. Ask yourself: *How can I work to make this happen?* It may be as simple as asking a student to share a special food or custom from their country of origin, to enrich the curriculum.

Thinking about consequences with the students

√ Discuss the consequences of breaking rules with your students, and remember that there are some natural consequences as well as imposed ones. For example, the natural consequence of students being repeatedly rude or disrespectful towards their peers is that they may be rejected by them, in addition to suffering a consequence imposed by school or class rules. A natural consequence of being off- task often is that they will probably not be able to keep up with the rest of the class or complete their work.

√ Under the teacher's direction, make allowances for different circumstances in setting rules (e.g. students must stay in their places during quiet seatwork, but are allowed to move around the room during activities). However, don't make so many variations that it becomes too complex for students to remember and for you to enforce.

√ Consider the consequences for appropriate behavior as well as inappropriate behavior, and let students know that there will be positive consequences (rewards) for observing rules as well as negative consequences for breaking them. Then make sure you deliver!

Setting goals for improvement in my work

Promoting positive behavior

The area I'm going to focus on:

The suggestion I'm going to use:

Time in which I'm going to try this suggestion:

How will I check on my progress?

What I noticed when I used the suggestion:

How will I include my supervisor in this goal-setting process?

CHAPTER 2: MAXIMIZING USE OF TIME

There are many demands upon your time as a paraeducator, but the main purpose of your work is supporting student achievement, and this is the area that must be given priority. This chapter contains suggestions for managing the time allocated to you for your work with students. You will find a whole section on transitions - movement between classes or activities - and how to best manage these transitions so that the least possible time is wasted on distractions, and the majority of time is dedicated to helping students succeed.

Have equipment and supplies available

Dealing with equipment and supplies can soak up an enormous amount of teaching and learning time. Consider each of these suggestions, and ask yourself whether you already incorporate them into your daily work, and if not, could you do so – to maximize the benefits to students of the time you spend with them.

⏰ Have "self-starter" activities available for the beginning of the day or the class session. These must be activities that are self-explanatory, or which the students know they can pick up and start on as soon as they come to the room or the workspace. This is to make sure that no time is wasted waiting for instructions. This also helps the students to get into the habit of being busy and engaged in useful activities. Such activities should be related to the topic of the work in which the students are about to engage, but be creative! Self-starter activities for the humanities and sciences can include crossword puzzles, easy quizzes, a drawing or design of a relevant item, word searches, or a compilation of relevant vocabulary lists. They can be completed by students individually or in pairs. If it's appropriate, you can include a competitive element as motivation.

⏰ If you are using several worksheets during a lesson, make certain that they are in the right order, to avoid confusion for the students, and time wasted.

⏰ Collate and staple pages of handouts before you distribute them to students.

⏰ Subject to your supervisor's approval, ask for student volunteers to help prepare materials for activities. Many students enjoy helping adults generally, for older students it gives them some insight into the work of a paraeducator as a potential career, and working informally with students on such tasks provides opportunities for you to develop your relationship with them.

⏰ Make extra copies of worksheets to use with students who "forget" their homework.

⏰ Plastic totes or crates may be helpful to store materials near to where they will be used. This certainly can save your time, but also makes the materials more easily accessible to students.

⏰ Each morning check your needed supplies such as marker pens, pencils, and stapler. Save time by having them at hand rather than looking for them during a teaching session. Have a small box or zip-lock pouch for such essentials.

⏰ Make certain you have enough extension cords and electrical adapters if you are using audio-visual equipment. Then test the equipment before you plan to use it, to make sure it works and so that you can use it confidently. Make sure that you set up close to an outlet.

Teaching students to manage their own time

In the early grades you can expect to tell students what to do next, or when to move from one activity to the next, and you generally manage their time in the classroom. However, as students move up through school, we teach them to manage their own time. Effective time management is a skill that will enhance success in life.

⏰ Set time management expectations for your students, e.g. "I'm going to give you 10 minutes to do this assignment. Spend about the first 3 minutes reading through the words, and the rest of the time answering the questions. I'll let you know when the first 3 minutes are up". This sets a model for the students to manage their own time, and while the pace you set will not suit all of them, it should help to make them more aware of how they work and the time they may need for different aspects of a task. As they become more aware, you can begin to include them in setting expectations, e.g. "I usually give you about 3 minutes to read the questions? Do you think that's enough? Or will you need a little longer?"

⏰ Help students to pace themselves by telling them how long an activity will take, e.g. "This assignment should take about 20 minutes. It looks short but it is quite difficult, so you'll need to give it the full time". This helps prevent students rushing to finish, giving the task insufficient attention, and therefore having to review or re- do their work – which can be very discouraging for them. It also reassures those students who feel they might be working too slowly.

⏰ Check with your teacher for meaningful extension activities for students who finish assignments early, to help them further develop the skills they have been practicing.

⏰ In this era of rapid changes in technology, it is still important that students develop skills such as clear communication, thoughtful reading, and the ability to ask productive questions. Model these skills for your students by pausing for reflection during reading passages or other activities, giving clear, concise information, and asking relevant and meaningful questions. These skills help you and the students put time to better use.

⏰ You will help students to pace their work if you sometimes set a kitchen timer as a signal to start work. (If you have the appropriate technology, such as an inter- active whiteboard, you can display a timer there.) Make sure you tell students how long the timer is set for, how much of the assignment needs to be finished when the timer goes off, and what they should do when they hear the timer - hand in their work, sit ready for feedback or review of the work, or move on to the next part.

Although speed is not the most important attribute for every task, and some students are naturally more able to think and recall information more quickly, giving them a certain advantage, you can introduce a competitive element occasionally if you feel the group would enjoy it.

Collection and correction of homework

This may not be one of your assigned responsibilities. However, if your supervising teacher has asked you to collect or correct homework, these suggestions will be helpful.

⏰ Some homework assignments can be checked with the whole class giving a choral response to the assigned items – this would include those with single, simple answers to a list of questions, or even spelling items. When the chorus weakens, make a note of the item for review. Students can circle the items they have worked incorrectly. If you also circulate as you ask for these responses, you can quickly see which concept or item of information students are having difficulty with that need to be re-taught.

⏰ If a student brings a homework assignment to class only partly completed, ask him or her to join the rest of the group to correct as much as is completed, and then instructions and move him/her to another part of the room to complete the remainder. Reinforce the student for what has been completed and for working quietly on the rest. Homework should not be associated with negative consequences.

⏰ If students have papers to submit at the end of a session, you can have them leave them on their desks and collect them during recess, rather than take up lesson time. Or you could have students turn them in (drop them in a tray or hand them to a designated student) as they leave the classroom.

⏰ Keep the homework-checking procedures to a 5-minute maximum. Then use the information you gain to decide whether you should re-teach concepts or if you can safely move on to new concepts. Remember to consult with your supervising teacher if you have concerns that you cannot deal with yourself, and to keep the teacher apprised of students' progress.

Beginning classwork with students' attention

Get students' attention before you begin teaching. Trying to talk while students are visiting is ineffective and may require you to repeat the information. It is also unfair to the students who are paying attention.

🔔 Encourage students to come to class on time by rewarding those who are punctual.

🔔 Be sure you get to class and work on time. By arriving on time you serve as a model for the behavior you expect of your students.

When the teacher establishes a schedule of the curricular subjects, check to see if you can post a copy where all students can see it. Then students know where they are in the schedule of the day.

Keep your schedule and/or lesson plan open on your desk or worktable, so that you know at a glance what your next activity will be. Set the example for students by being ready to begin sessions promptly.

Use a hand-puppet to get and keep young students' attention. Younger students especially are likely to pay close attention if the puppet does the "teaching" and they can be given the puppet to hold as they respond to your questions. This would disrupt the flow of the lesson if you constantly passed the puppet around.
Using this for the review time at the end of the teaching session can keep the students focused until the end of the session, and it maintains novelty value.

If you use a verbal prompt to get students' attention, try to avoid using words that seem to encourage inappropriate behavior. For example, if you use the word "Go!" to signal students to move, they may associate it with a race and feel that speed is the most important factor encouraging them to run to the next activity.
Instead, use phrases such as "Are you ready?" and then when you are sure you have their attention: "You may now go quietly to your next class/activity".

Teach your students an attention-getter, such as a short hand-clapping rhythm. This saves you from having to raise your voice above theirs, and ensures that hands as well as minds are focused and ready for instructions. Depending on the age of the students you may just raise one hand in the air, hold both hands up and wiggle all your fingers, or place a finger on your lips in the sign of a whisper or shush.

When all of your students are paying attention, briefly praise the group for their attentiveness, but be sure that the praise is specific, e.g. "Thank-you for being ready to start so quickly", rather than a general "Good, now we can start". This focuses their attention on the desired behavior and is an easy way to remind them how to behave appropriately.

To get students attention at the beginning of the class you can use index cards with review questions written on them. If you distribute the cards as students are sitting down, it gives them something work-oriented to focus on as the group is arriving and getting settled.

Facilitating transitions

There are two major types of transitions:
1. student transitions, e.g. moving from one activity to the next, getting a drink of water, or handing in assignments; and
2. educator transitions, e.g. collecting students from another room, or gathering materials for the next activity.

You need to carefully think out and prepare for both of these types of transitions, to ensure that students know where they should be going next, or what they should be doing, and to ensure that you are well prepared for change.

Appropriate behavior must be taught. Every time there's a transition from one activity to another, tell the students what behavior you expect to see – that is, where they need to go next, what they will need to take with them, and what they should do with the materials from the current activity. And don't forget to compliment those students who live up to that expectation.

Have activities on hand for students who finish their work before it is time to transition the group to the next activity. This may be as simple as an item to color on the worksheet the student is completing (for younger children), but you can use whatever you think will be motivating for your students.

To settle students back to work quickly after a break (such as recess), prepare a short activity which you place on their desks during the break, and which is therefore waiting for them on their return. Keep it short or allow them just a few minutes to work on it – they can finish it the next time they're working with you if necessary.

When students finish a task or an assignment early, reinforce those who find something appropriate to do unprompted while they are waiting to transition to the next activity, for example free choice of reading materials or activity books, or a chance to catch up on other unfinished assignments.

A few minutes before you change to another activity, let students know that a transition is about to take place. Then make certain students are attending before you give directions for the transitions. This is particularly important for younger students and those on the autistic spectrum, who need clear structure and clear expectations, and generally dislike the unexpected interruption of an activity. It is worth noting that students on the autistic spectrum can also become distressed if you do not finish an activity at the stated or expected time – a good reminder to be punctual both beginning and ending an activity.

Make it clear to your students that they should only bring essential items with them when they come to work with you. This will save the time removing distracting items or reminding students to keep them out of sight.

Give some thought to how many students really need to be involved in certain activities. For example, roll call. Do you need to take up all of the students' time to call roll? Or could you just have students get straight down to work and use a seating chart to call a silent roll? Or could one of the students be assigned to this task? If several students are interested in participating in completing the roll, you can put them on a rota, or use this as a motivator for appropriate student behavior at the beginning of the teaching session.

Decide in advance how you want students to move from one activity or another. Should they "line up" and wait for your direction? Or can they move independently? Consider the amount of disruptive, inappropriate behavior that occurs with each procedure and choose whichever seems the least disruptive. Older children in particular prefer to move around unsupervised, but younger children also like to feel they're 'like the big students' and can therefore be encouraged to behave appropriately and be allowed greater independence and reduced supervision (provided they are in a safe environment). You will find that the rule will vary according to the group you are working with, as some students will be more or less willing and able to move around the school independently, no matter what their age.

For students who are easily distracted as they move around the room or school, a little physical prompt is useful. If you're walking with them, simply placing a hand lightly on their shoulder will help them to keep pace with you and not run ahead.

✝ Appoint a 'leader' for a group of students who need to move from one area of the school to another, with the rule that no one is to walk ahead of the leader. If you are accompanying the students, it is generally better for you to walk behind them, as you can more easily check on the students from the rear.

✝ If you have a student who finds it particularly difficult to follow procedures, privately remind them of appropriate behavior. Then make sure you briefly praise them when they do what is required.

✝ If students have to wait in line and are becoming restless, engage them in a directed activity. This is a great opportunity to review, and keeps them from becoming overly disruptive. You'll find some examples of suitable activities in the box.

Short activities to engage students while they are waiting in line

Counting - in chorus or with each student taking a turn – in 2s, 5s, 10s, or whatever number is suitable to the abilities of the group (it could be counting multiples of a number such as 16 or even 509 for more able students)

Spelling – either items from the current spelling list, families of words such as those ending in *–tion*, or associated words such as countries

Singing – songs which assist learning (such as counting songs) or just fun songs the students are all likely to know; one paraeducator sang Christmas songs with high school students in the off-season, which they enjoyed all the more because it was unexpected

---

> *Clapping* – have students repeat rhythms that you – or one of the students - has clapped

🪧 When students move from whole group instruction to smaller group sessions, train them to bring all of the materials they will need. Even though they may stay in the same classroom this is an example of a transition, which needs to be as seamless as possible. Don't allow transition periods to interrupt the flow of the lesson.

🪧 If you plan several activities during one lesson period, give some thought to the many different materials you and the students may need, and the implications for transitions as well as organization. Will too much time be spent changing from one activity to the other? Try to strike a balance. KISS (Keep It Simple) is a good general rule.

🪧 Have students bring only necessary materials for each separate activity.

🪧 Think ahead what you will do about interruptions to your lessons, such as PA announcements, so that you can quickly transition back to the lesson. Instruct students whether you want them to carry on with their work while you deal with the interruption, or wait momentarily. You can let them know that you need to deal with the interruption, but will do it as quickly as possible. This shows what your priorities are.

🪧 Summarize the main points of a lesson before moving on to another activity, so that students realize that you are bringing the activity to a close and they will be transitioning to a new activity.

Setting goals for improvement in my work

Maximizing Use of Time

The area I'm going to focus on:

The suggestion I'm going to use:

Time in which I'm going to try this suggestion:

How will I check on my progress?

What I noticed when I used the suggestion:

How will I include my supervisor in this goal-setting process?

CHAPTER 3: MEETING LEARNER NEEDS

There are many ways of delivering instruction, but effective instructional strategies should have the following components:

1. a check that students have the knowledge and skills required to understand the material you are about to cover;

2. presentation of new material in small steps;

3. careful monitoring of student understanding as you give them guided practice in the material taught;

4. independent practice activities where students work without close supervision; and

5. regular cumulative reviews.

This becomes a teaching cycle, as the reviews can also serve to check whether students have the prerequisite skills for the next concepts to be taught.

As a paraeducator your main task may be to supervise guided or independent practice, or to conduct reviews, rather than present new material. However, if students have not understood what has been taught by the teacher, you may need to re-teach material. You will find the sections on *checking current knowledge and skills*, and *presentation of material* most helpful. It is also important that you understand where your contribution to the process of teaching and learning fits into the whole.

Checking for current knowledge and skills

We check students' current skills and knowledge because there are almost always pre-requisites for new material we present to students. A pre-requisite is something that we need to have, or know, before we can begin the current task, or engage with the next step in the learning process. It is the foundation on which we build new knowledge. There may be several prerequisites for some tasks or learning. For example, for a child to be able to read, they must understand that the words on a page have meaning, that text is read from left to right (in English), that there are consistent sound-letter correspondences which will enable them to de-code the sequences of letters which make up words and sentences. Likewise in their later school years, they will need to have an understanding of algebra before they can engage with calculus, or a basic understanding of arithmetic and algebra before they can study statistics.

√ When checking for prerequisite skills, use a variety of methods to get the students' attention and keep their interest: play games, or review memory tricks, rather than always just asking questions.

√ Ask students to give a short summary of what they remember from the previous lesson. Acknowledge and praise correct information; identify for the students those areas which have not been remembered accurately, reassuring them that you will be covering those in today's session.

√ Ask your group of students to give as many facts as they can remember from the previous lesson. To make it fun, award points or other rewards, even for the smallest piece of accurate information, so that all students will be willing to make contributions. You could also divide the group into two teams and have each one make contributions, or ask each other questions (which they must know the answer to!) You will find more ideas on how to check for prerequisite skills in the box.

Checking for prerequisites

- ask questions

- show a series of pictures or illustrations that relate to the prerequisite
    skills and use them as prompts for students to tell you what they
    remember from a previous session, or already know about the topic

- use 4 or 5 objects in the same way to prompt students to recall
    or provide information about a topic

- assign a student to provide a review of material from a previous session,
    and have the other students add what they remember after the
    student has given the review

- use flashcards

√ Make sure that you have taught students *how* to do what you have asked of them, not just the content of the lesson, e.g. don't assume they have prerequisite knowledge such as what a report is, or how to draw a diagram.

Presenting new material

New material is literally what it says – material which the students have not yet covered. This is generally the responsibility of the teacher. For some students, 'new' material may not be entirely unfamiliar. It is one of the major challenges of teaching, to engage children in the prescribed curriculum when they come to school from a wide variety of backgrounds and with differing interests and abilities.

√ New material should be taught in small steps to assure that students understand each concept before moving on to the next one. There is no precise measure for a 'small step' – it is essentially the amount of new information that a student can handle.

√ The level of language used in presentations (vocabulary, sentence structure, etc.) must be consistent with students' levels of understanding and rate of learning. Use words students will understand, and clear, simple language for presenting ideas.

√ Make sure you provide a clear definition of new terms, and give students examples of those terms used in sentences, to clarify and illustrate their meaning.

√ Explain to students the purpose or goal of a lesson, together with a rationale, or reason, for it. They will be more willing to engage in an activity when they have some idea what to expect and know why it is important.

√ Keep good eye contact with students, unless this is inappropriate to their home culture.

√ If you use technology make sure it relates directly to the subject matter. Students should realize what they are to learn from it rather than just being entertained.

√ Try to relate new information to students' current knowledge. This helps them remember the new information and to see connections with other subject areas.

√ Help students understand how new information relates to their lives. Ask them to give examples of situations in which the information would be applicable and useful. This will help them remember the information and will generally make it more meaningful for them.

√ With elementary or young students use students' names in examples or illustrations. This gives them a sense that the example applies directly to them, and helps to keep their attention focused on the lesson material.

√ If you are working with a student at the computer, minimize the window you are working in so that distractions are at a minimum.

Advance Organizers

Advance organizers give students a 'heads-up' on what to expect from a teaching session. Advance organizers are also found in newspaper/magazine articles – in fact almost any piece of writing has an advance organizer in the introduction. It helps the reader know what to expect, and hopefully piques their interest enough to tempt them to read the whole article. An advance organizer at the beginning of an activity serves the same function – and ideally is presented in a way which draws students in and engages them with the content.

√ You can write the outline of an activity on the whiteboard, and check off the items as they are covered, so that students can follow along more easily with the flow of ideas and information. This will also help if the teacher asks you to conduct the review at the end of a lesson. An outline should only have 3 or 4 items at the most, as it is difficult for students to keep track when the outline has more than this number of items.

√ Another method of providing an outline is to use a mind-map or spider diagram. For some students this is more logical and understandable than a linear list of topics. Here's an example of a mind map:

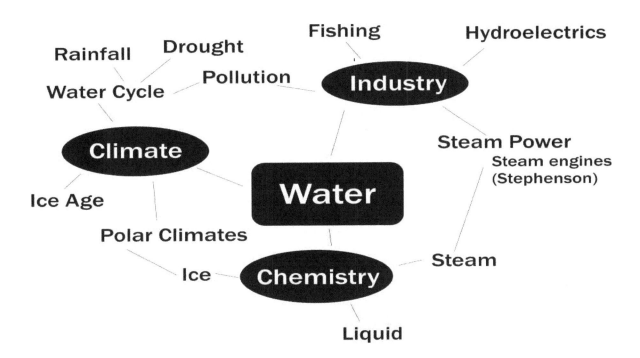

√ If the school allows it, try recording an activity so you can check how well you follow the prepared outline. If students are aware that you are recording the lesson, they may act out at first, but you can explain your purpose. Repeated recordings will reduce the novelty value, and students will learn to ignore the equipment. (Be sure that recording is allowed in the classroom, to minimize issues of confidentiality.)

√ When new concepts are introduced to students with a number of points to cover, write them on a 3 x 5 card. This card will also be useful when they review the information, at the end of the lesson, or at the end of the week. You can also make brief notes in pencil about student response to the information on a card – whether you feel they should cover that information again, because they don't appear to have quite grasped its full meaning, for example.

Presentation styles

Whether teachers are presenting new material, or you are reviewing that material, the presentation style is critical. Students will react not only to the content but also to the way in which content is presented. You don't have to be like a magician, always producing tricks and entertaining students. But the extent to which you show enthusiasm in your voice and approach to the content will have a direct effect on the extent to which students engage with that content. It is also important to vary your presentation so that it doesn't become routine and predictable.

√ Be precise and clear in your choice of vocabulary so students hear the facts: avoid using ambiguous terms such as *almost, a couple, some,* and *pretty much*. For example, if you told students "A few years ago, some men in the government decided that..."   they would have no sense of how long ago or how many people. You could be talking about the men who formed the Constitution more than 200 years ago, or something that happened this century.

√ Express yourself in a confident manner. Students will have more confidence in what you say and in their own learning. It's easier to do this if you are confident about what you are doing and saying, so make sure you are well informed, and if you don't know the answer to a question, say so, and tell the student you will find out.

√ Speak at a volume that assures you can easily be heard by the group you are working with, but vary your voice tone and volume to make your presentation more appealing for students. This is particularly important for the youngest students, as we tend to exaggerate facial expressions and tone of voice in order to communicate ideas more clearly for them – especially when telling stories. However even for the oldest students, variation in volume and tone makes for more interesting presentation.

√ Using effective strategies for meeting learning needs is basically a 3-step process:

1. You demonstrate a correct response;
2. You prompt the student to respond correctly with your help; and
3. The student responds alone.

For example if you were reading with a student and there was a new word in the text, you would first sound out the word, then have the student sound out the word with you, and then ask the student to read the word on his/her own. If you were helping a student with computer keyboard skills, you would use the procedure with the student watching you, then guide the student to use the procedure, then have the student show you the procedure independently. With younger students, you might say: 'I do'
            'We do'   'You do'

√ If material appears to be too difficult for students, inform the teacher. Do not reduce the level of difficulty of material yourself. When the level of difficulty is just right, presentations can be brisk and interesting for students. A small amount of material successfully covered gives students more confidence and they are better prepared to move on to new material in the next lesson.

Checking for student understanding

We use the term *checking* here to mean *keeping track* or *monitoring*. We have avoided using the terms *evaluating* or *assessing* as these tend to be the teacher's responsibility and are associated with more formal testing of student progress. The importance of checking for student understanding cannot be stressed too strongly, because it helps us understand where students are in the learning process. Here we encourage you to think more carefully about how you can monitor students.

Watching for clues

√ When you ask a question, if you get no response, re-phrase the question.

√ As students are working independently, watch to see if they seem to know what to do. You can usually tell by expressions and body language whether they are actively engaged with their work, or if they are frustrated and confused.

√ Be aware that when students don't participate, it may mean that they don't understand. Crying, misbehavior, or saying the work is boring are warning signs that the work may be too difficult for the student.

√ Ask your supervising teacher if you can observe while she or he teaches, so that you can watch and learn from how s/he asks questions and monitors student understanding. You may also find it helpful to write down the techniques that are used so that you can try them.

Effective questions

√ Questions, questions, questions! Ask as many as possible to give more students more opportunities to respond – and so that you have a better idea of whether students have understood.

√ There is an art to asking effective questions. Write down the questions you are going to ask students prior to an activity. Consider the variety of possible answers for that question and how you would respond to them.

√ Make sure the questions you ask are not really two (or more) questions tacked together. Ask only one question at a time. It is less confusing for students and gives you a clearer idea of what students have understood. Several separate questions are much easier to answer than one complex question with several parts.

√ Ask both high-level questions (Why? What do you think? How?) and low-level questions (What? Who? How many? When?). Low level questions check knowledge of facts, and high-level questions require students to analyze and synthesize information.

Low level questions:

- begin with words such as What? Who? How many? and generally have only one right answer

High level questions:

- begin with words or phrases such as Why? What do you think? or How? and can have many right answers. In some cases there is no wrong answer.

√ Don't forget to include discussion questions that make students apply and analyze information. Even very young children can do this if the information is at an appropriate level (e.g. ask why they think the character in the story is acting in a particular way, or how they think the story will end).

√ If you want students to practice responses to low-level factual questions individually or in pairs, you can use index cards. Cut a piece of colored plastic the same size as the card. Then write a question on the card with a black or dark pen, but write the answer in a felt-tip pen the same color as the plastic. When you staple the plastic onto the card, the question will show through, but the answer will be invisible, so students can read the question, give an answer, and then lift the film to check if they were correct. You could also use these cards to get oral feedback from the group or class.

√ Students often like to make up questions for the rest of the class. This could be orally for younger students and written for older students, and should be encouraged. They may not know the exact answer themselves, but their questions will give you an idea of the level of their understanding. They may also prefer to make up the questions in pairs or groups, rather than on their own.

√ Write questions on slips of paper, put them in a jar and have students draw them one at a time. If you put the questions back in the jar to be pulled more than once, the answers become more familiar every time they occur. Less able students will be reassured to know that they have a good chance of getting a repeat question.

√ Consider the cultural implications of questions. For example, if you ask *When was the civil war?* there could be several different answers depending on the background and origins of the students. Many countries have had civil wars, so each student could answer the question in relation to their own country of origin.

√ When students have answered a question you have asked to monitor their understanding, move on quickly to the next point, so that you don't break the flow of the lesson or lose students' attention.

Student responses

One of the important aspects of prompting student responses is to use variety, so here we provide a wide range of suggestions for how to conduct activities which include student response. Alert students to which mode or method you are using at any given time, so that they know what to expect from the activity.

√ Students need to feel comfortable and secure before they will venture to make a verbal response in a group setting. Have them work in pairs to get used to sharing their ideas before having them give a response to the whole class.

√ *Think-Pair-Share* is a useful strategy for engaging all students simultaneously and for providing them with peer support, before they respond to questions. Ask them to *Think* (on their own) about a particular aspect of the lesson material (e.g. why...? or what...?), then have them *Pair* up with another student and exchange ideas. Finally have one student from each pair *Share* their ideas with the rest of the group.

√ When you check for student understanding, you can make it into a one-student race. Have students make a note of how long it takes them to finish the task, and the next time they can compete against their own time. Although speed isn't always the most important measure of learning, skills such as times tables and other math facts need to be automatic (over-learned). Working at speed shows whether student answers are spontaneous, or whether they are still working laboriously through a calculation.

√ To help students develop automatic responses to low level questions, encourage them to give the first answer that comes into their head. This gives a clearer idea of whether they have the answers at their finger-tips (that is, whether the material is sufficiently well understood/learned that they have instant recall, so their response is automatic), and helps less confident students get out of the habit of pondering over every question before risking giving an answer.

√ If you're working with a group of students and need to get a lot of group responses, try this idea. Give each student a cube (sides about 3 inches long). Choose 3 colors and color opposite sides of the cube the same color (or stick squares of those colors on opposite sides of the cube). Then use the colors to represent different answers (e.g. yes, no, I don't know; or true, false, not sure). When you ask a question, make sure the students know which answer each color represents and have them hold up the cube so that the color of their answer is facing you. (That same color will be facing them too, if you've colored opposite sides the same so they'll know that what they see is also what you see.) Using colors in this way rather than words, it is easier for you to tell at a glance whether the group has understood, especially with a large group of students. You will need to practice using these cubes, as you need to practice any other classroom procedure, but once students are familiar with using this strategy, it won't distract from the activity.

√ Call on students by name to respond to question or to read words. They like the personal note, and it helps them to understand that they need to be personally involved in the current activity.

√ Don't always accept "I don't know". Once you allow one student to say 'I don't know' that may be the only answer you are offered. So press students for a response – it helps students pay attention, and gets them used to the idea that there is no shame in giving a wrong answer, and that trying to answer will at least get them some feedback. Then praise them for taking risks and having the courage to try even if they're not confident that their answer is right.

√ Take opportunities to make students feel successful. Even if a response is not entirely accurate, acknowledge the parts of it which are correct and then go over the parts which are not.

√ Allow several hands to go up before asking for a response, rather than asking the first student who raises a hand. This shows students that they have time to think about an answer, and will get a chance to respond even if they're not the fastest thinker in the group. Otherwise those who know they are slower may give up because they quickly learn that the faster thinkers will have given the answer before they can think of it themselves.

√ The length of time you wait for an answer to a question will depend upon the difficulty of the question. For example, quick-fire questions and short, sharp answers are appropriate for low-level questions which just require factual answers, but more time should be given for thought on high-level questions which require students to analyze and think through problems.

√ It is also important to vary the amount of time you allow for students to think and respond, because you want answers from all the students, not just the fastest thinkers.

√ For questions with one-word answers or a number, students could write their answer in large writing on a piece of paper or card, and hold it up so that you can scan the whole group quickly, and know whether you need to review material or move on.

√ You can write questions on cards, hand them out to students, and have them read the question out loud and give an answer. This distributes questions randomly, but students often like the "chance" element of not knowing what question they may get. If you sometimes allow students to work in pairs on a card/question, they have the opportunity to discuss their answer and pool their knowledge before giving an answer. If the answer they give is correct, they can both feel good about it; if the answer is incorrect neither of them is alone in being 'wrong.'

√ Have each student write his/her name on a card, collect the cards and use them to call on students for responses. When every student has been called on, you can start over, or shuffle the cards so that they don't know when their turn will next come around. This helps students stay alert and focused on the lesson.

√ Remember that students can be asked to demonstrate a skill (e.g. dribbling a ball, or mixing paint colors) to show their levels of understanding – responses do not always have to be word-based. You can ask them to demonstrate to the rest of the class, or just to you if they feel more comfortable that way. This also gives them another opportunity to practice.

√ Use a timer or stopwatch to set the limits for some activities. Students of all ages like to race the clock, and they can try to beat their own time or performance when you repeat the activity, rather than trying to beat another student's time or performance. You can use this for math facts, or for helping students to increase their reading speed by timing words read per minute. It can help students to make their answers more spontaneous and automatic, which is particularly important for basic skills.

Helping students remember

√ Teach your students mnemonics to help them remember important facts or procedures. For example:

Never Eat Shredded Wheat (N, E, S, W - the order of the points of the compass)

Sammy's Old Horse Carries Aunt Hannah to Old Alabama. This one's for trigonometry: SOH: sine = opposite/hypotenuse, CAH: cosine = adjacent/hypotenuse; TOA; tangent = opposite/adjacent.

HOME = names of the Great Lakes (Huron, Ontario, Michigan, Erie) FACE

= the names of the musical notes in the spaces of the treble clef.

Denominator lives Downstairs (The denominator is the bottom figure of a fraction).

Dolly Parton fractions are improper fractions - heavier on the top!

Think of **S**trawberry **S**hortcake to remind you that there are 2 s's in de**ss**ert.

Emphasize the rhyme in such things as 6 x 8 = 48

√ Students like to learn 'tricks' that can help them find the right answer to a question. For example, in math, multiplying by 11. Up to 9 x 11 the answers are just double digits of the number you're multiplying, so 3 x 11 = 33 and 5 x 11 = 55. But students can play with much larger double-digit numbers when they come to know the pattern: split the number, add the two digits together, and insert the total of the two digits in the middle. So 15 x 11 = 165 (1 + 5 = 6, which you insert between the 1 and 5). Although this method only works this simply when the two digits come to less than 10, once they have mastered the pattern it will be a useful exercise for them to explore the new pattern for numbers where the digits add up to more than 10.

Did you know that you can easily remember the 9 times table by using your fingers? For example, for 3 x 9 hold up all 10 fingers, count on your right hand: 1, 2, 3, and hold the 3rd finger down. What you have remaining is the answer: 2 fingers to the left of the finger that's down, and 7 fingers in total, giving 27.

Reinforcing and encouraging students

When students behave or respond appropriately, you need to let them know, so that they can do it again. A focus on positive behavior is likely to increase the behavior you want to see more often. This is more effective than only correcting inappropriate behavior.

√ Use specific statements to let a student know what he did for the praise - not just "good" or "great" but what he did that was good. This way he can remember what he did and continue to do it without you telling him every day.

√ Students really like it when their name is mentioned as they are doing a good job. It helps keep them wanting to be on task.

√ Make an effort to vary the ways in which you acknowledge students' efforts, by listing as many different words or phrases you can think of that express appreciation. And then don't forget to use them. You'll find some suggestions to start you off in the box.

<table>
<tr><td colspan="3">Short phrases to acknowledge students' efforts
(complete the phrases with the specific action you are praising)</td></tr>
<tr><td>Terrific...!</td><td>Good thinking</td><td>Brilliant idea!</td></tr>
<tr><td>Absolutely</td><td>Thank-you for...</td><td>Very impressive...</td></tr>
<tr><td>You got that right.</td><td>That's the idea</td><td>Nice writing!</td></tr>
<tr><td>Good for you</td><td>Good observation</td><td></td></tr>
</table>

√ Use physical signs of approval, such as:

| thumbs up | a pat on the back | okay sign | handshake |
| high five | silent applause | a wink | |

√ If students show an interest in a topic that is very different from the one that you are discussing, you need to decide whether to tell them you may give them the opportunity to talk about that topic at another time, but that you do not wish them to get sidetracked for the time being. Or you may choose to pursue the topic, as it is always very motivating for students to be able to pursue a topic of choice. This, of course, is subject to your supervising teacher's approval. But if you choose to postpone the discussion of the topic students have shown an interest in, don't forget to keep your word and come back to the topic if you can. If your teacher tells you that she or he will be covering that topic at some future time, pass that information on to the students so that they know you have not forgotten their request.

Summing up

Lesson summaries need to be very clear and precise and should be thought out carefully beforehand. They offer an opportunity to re-state the main points covered in the session, and shouldn't include new ideas. Asking questions at the end of a presentation, serves to summarize and determine whether students have understood. These questions can be phrased as if the students are making a self- assessment of their understanding, by stating it this way: "Ask yourself, what do I know now about...?" Each point from the lesson can be covered with a question.

Students can also be given an opportunity to ask you questions about points they do not feel confident about.

√ Ask yourself what information you most want students to remember. Then stay focused on that information – don't let yourself be sidetracked - and keep the amount of information appropriate to the age and ability levels of the students.

√ If students were confused about any particular points during the initial presentation of material, highlight those points as you present the summary of the lesson, and then check for understanding.

√ At the end of one activity or lesson, set the stage for the next day's lesson or activity, so that students can know what to expect. If you mention the following day's topic in an interesting way, students will look forward to your next lesson.

Giving guided practice

Guided practice is practice *with immediate feedback*. This is a particularly appropriate role for paraeducators, and most paraeducators spend the majority of their instructional time giving guided practice to students. That means you have to be available to let students know whether their responses are correct or incorrect, as they practice new skills or knowledge. This enables the student to make adjustments to their performance so that their practice brings them closer and closer to being correct – or to being correct more and more often. Otherwise students can practice errors, and those errors then get established in the students' minds. There are two examples in the box on the next page of how Guided Practice can help students as they acquire new skills.

Guided Practice: Example 1

Content area: Art

Skill: brush strokes

The paraeducator asks the student to produce a particular brush-stroke, while the paraeducator observes. If the paraeducator sees that the student is holding the brush correctly for that stroke, he/she confirms that for the student (e.g. *Yes, see how holding the brush further away from the bristles gives you better control when you're stippling).* If the student holds the brush incorrectly, the paraeducator can indicate that the brush should be held differently (e.g. *try holding the brush further away from the bristles – it'll give you better control),* show the student the correct grip and demonstrate the stroke using that grip, and ask the student to imitate the grip and make the appropriate brushstrokes. If the student imitates the grip correctly, the paraeducator should acknowledge the improved grip (*Good – that's a much better grip)*; if not, the paraeducator should provide more specific instruction (*Try leaving at least 4cms between your fingers and the metal)* and check on the student again after a few minutes.

Guided Practice: Example 2

Content area: Modern Languages (Spanish)

Skill: using prepositions

The paraeducator has placed a small table on the desk at the front of the class, and has a book in his hand. Placing the book on the table, the paraeducator asks: *Donde esta el libro?* and gives the response, *El libro es sopra la mesa.* He then asks the same question of three students, repeating the phrase, *Si, el libro es sopra la mesa* if the students give the correct response, and *No, el libro es sopra la mesa* if a student gives an incorrect preposition or otherwise mistaken answer. He then moves the book under the table and asks the question again, directing the question to different students (by name), confirming the response if the student is hesitant, but responding with only *Si, muy buen* when a student gives a correct, confident response. In this way he covers a variety of prepositions by moving the book *behind, in front of, at the side of* the table, etc.

√ When you want to illustrate a point or guide students through practice examples, have several examples ready in case students have difficulty relating to the first one you use.

√ Give students as much help and support as they need to accomplish a task. For example, some students are afraid to be creative because they feel they have no talent, so if you ask them to draw a bird, show them the basic body parts and how they can change the size, shape and proportions of each one to make their own unique drawing. Those who feel confident will automatically make their own versions, and those who are less confident can still produce something unique.

√ When you give examples to illustrate a point, be sure to use examples that are clear and unambiguous, so that the examples serve their purpose and do not confuse students. This includes only using vocabulary and contexts the students are familiar with, otherwise they will not be able to create a picture in their minds to help them visualize your meaning or apply the concept you are discussing.

√ When you review more difficult concepts, use concrete examples to illustrate your point - the more difficult the concept, the more concrete the examples initially need to be.

√ If you're reading with a student, offer to read every other sentence. It moves the story along faster, so that it's easier to maintain the student's interest, and the student can follow as you read and therefore model the words, especially items of vocabulary that may be new to the student.

√ In all your presentations and practice examples, start with the simplest ideas and then move on to the more complex.

√ Keep learning objectives in mind as you make decisions about whether students have understood well enough to be allowed to move on from guided practice to independent practice.

√ Before moving students from guided practice to independent practice make sure that they are answering correctly at a high rate, otherwise they will practice errors as they work without immediate feedback.

√ Pose problems for your students, rather than always asking them to give facts or figures. This makes them apply the information that they have learned. However, you should make sure that they know the facts first, as applying facts is more complex and demanding, and they will not be able to apply facts they have not yet learned.

√ If students are getting only about half of the answers to your questions right, check these things: Are your questions clear enough that students can understand them? and Do the questions relate directly to the material you've been teaching? or Are you asking for extras that you really haven't covered?

√ Use a variety of methods of guided practice to suit a variety of learning styles and topics. Some students will find it easier to talk through an answer rather than writing it down, and some topics lend themselves more to demonstration rather than a written response. Sometimes you might like to give students alternatives and let them choose which mode of response they would prefer.

√ If some students seem to be having more difficulty than others, use an alternative method for re-teaching, such as having another student who has understood explain the concept. This gives the able student the opportunity to practice, and prevents him/her from getting bored by listening to a repeat of what is already understood, and it gives the slower students a change, perhaps a slightly different perspective from which to grasp the concept.

Setting goals and expectations for work

We often think of goals as long-term – skills to be acquired or curriculum content to be covered over the course of the school year or semester. However, goals can be set for weekly or daily work, and even for individual teaching sessions. They may relate to academic work or behavior.

√ Use visual reminders and motivators for students when setting instructional or behavioral goals. This could take the form of a bookmark or graph on which they chart their progress. Older students will be able to chart scores and timings, and younger students can color in pictures or symbols, or earn stickers.

√ Make sure you know the requirements of assignments in terms of accuracy, length, neatness, and type of materials to be used, and the date when assignments are due. This allows you to pass the information along to the students correctly.

√ If you are unsure of a procedure (for example in math or science), make a point of checking with the teacher. If the teacher is not available and you need to make a decision for the students, make sure you inform the teacher as soon as possible what that decision was, so that the teacher is prepared when the assignment is handed in.

√ When the teacher sets a goal for students be sure to model a good example of that goal. For example, if you want students to read with expression, make sure that when you read to students you vary your intonation, speed and volume; if you want to emphasize how important reading is, let students see you reading - when it's their reading time, you can sometimes sit and read a book too.

√ When you work with a group of students on a task, outline what you expect to cover with them during that session: what they can expect of you, and what you in turn expect of them.

√ Help students to manage their workload by breaking major goals or assignments into smaller units, and setting themselves timelines for accomplishing each step.
Even young children can be helped to do this, e.g. "Let's get the story written before recess and then you can illustrate it when you come back to class". For older students who may be sitting important examinations, this is especially important if they need to respond to a set number of questions – they need to learn to limit the time they spend on any one question.

√ Students can set their own goals for what they would like to achieve during a lesson period. Students of all ages can do this, and even if they are wildly inaccurate at first, they will soon learn to be more realistic with practice, and be able to set themselves targets that are attainable but challenging.

√ Remember that you will have to set expectations for behavior as well as for assignments. If you work with a group, remind them of your expectations while they work with you, which may be the same as when they work with the teacher, or may be slightly different for group work.

Supervising independent practice

Independent practice is exactly what is says: students are given opportunities to practice using skills or knowledge independently, or without direct supervision. Typically the paraeducator role in supervising independent practice may be restricted to collecting homework, or circulating while students complete a task relating to material they have already been taught and guided through. At secondary level this may be a study hall. You will note that we call this section *Supervising independent practice,* which means that you are present with them, but you are generally supervising the activity, and only working directly and continuously with a student if they request your help, or if you can see that they are struggling.

√ When students are working independently on assignments, their work should be fairly accurate. The rate of accuracy must be higher than during guided practice because you will not be available to provide constant feedback. Students should not be given independent practice assignments unless you are sure that they can attain this success rate, otherwise they will be practicing errors.

√ Independent practice can be drills, games or enrichment activities, which students can complete independently.

√ Independent practice could also be an application task such as fieldwork in the school grounds to apply math concepts.

√ Be aware that as students engage in independent practice, their responses should become more fluent and spontaneous.

√ Help students to see that independent practice helps them to develop fluency. For example, as they practice their multiplication tables, they will no longer have to waste time calculating the math facts in their head, but will be able to move on to applying them and learning new skills. This applies to so many areas such as playing a musical instrument, finding where their fingers are on the computer keyboard, or developing sports skills. Think how competent students generally are with texting – because they have voluntarily engaged in extensive independent practice!

√ Point out to students that their confidence is increasing as they demonstrate their growing expertise.

√ If you have extra papers left from an assignment, keep them where they are accessible to students. The teacher may offer extra credit to students who voluntarily complete extra assignments of their choice when they have finished required work.

Monitoring work

We monitor student work for two reasons. First, so that we know whether they are learning, that is, whether they are gaining the skills, knowledge and understanding we are assigned to teach them. Second, we monitor student work in order to evaluate whether our teaching has been effective. These are essentially two sides of the same coin, because we are looking at the results of the teaching and learning process from two angles: have the students gained in skills? and did the methods used appear to facilitate or hinder that process?

√ You can help students monitor their own progress or accuracy. You should check occasionally whether their record keeping has been honest and accurate, and praise them when you find that they have been keeping an honest and accurate record.

√ Help students self-monitor by for example writing a list of assignments and checking off each one as it is completed. For younger students you can write the list (or use graphics to represent each task). You can also teach them to break assignments or tasks down into their component parts, so that they can check each of the parts off as they complete them. (There is an example of a task broken down in this way in the box on the next page.) To begin with you may have to remind them to cross off each one as it is finished, but they will soon get into the habit of doing it for themselves.

Example of a task broken down into its components parts: Writing a letter

Write a letter to a local government official to express satisfaction or gratitude for some facility or event in the local community.
Remember:
- begin with your address at top right
- write the date under your address
- write the name and address of the local government official on the left
- leave one line empty
- begin 'Dear Mr/Mrs... ' (use their surname)
- start a new line for the main part of your letter (expressing satisfaction or
        gratitude for the local facility or event)
- leave one line empty
- finish with 'Yours Faithfully'
- sign your name underneath 'Yours Faithfully'

√ Give each student a small book to write down assignments and when they are due. When the assignments are completed you can initial, or place a sticker on the page.

√ If you are monitoring students who are working independently, such as on a worksheet, it may help students to pace their work if you mark off a section of the worksheet and have them raise their hand for your feedback when they reach the end of the marked section. Those who lack confidence or who are hesitant can be reassured that their work is accurate, and you can correct errors before students practice too many of them.

√ Speak to individual students about their work and how it is progressing. Ask what schedule they have set themselves for completing assignments. In this way, you acknowledge that they have control over the pace and organization of their work, and encourage independence.

√ In your small group with students sitting around a desk or table, assign a group captain and put him/her "in charge" of keeping group members working. You can change the captain each day, so each student has a turn, and give bonus points or some other incentive/reward for keeping the group on task.

√ For tasks such as listening to students read or checking homework completion, keep a set of index cards, one for each student. As you check with students or listen to them read, put their cards to the back or bottom of the pile, then call on the student whose card is next. In this way, no matter what order the cards are in, you make sure that you regularly see every student. A set of cards like this can be easily kept together with a clip and hung on a hook near your desk or workspace.

Conducting reviews

Reviews complete the instructional cycle, and provide the basis for a new cycle of teaching and learning, as they establish what students have learned and if concepts need to be re-taught. Thus reviews are essentially a check for pre-requisite skills and knowledge, but we include both *reviews* and a *check for pre-requisite skills* in the learning cycle, because typically the *review* finishes up one teaching session, and the *check for pre-requisite skills* starts up a new teaching session, and establishes whether the students have remembered what was covered in the last session.

Teachers conduct larger reviews at end of unit, semester and year, to determine the next level of teaching. As the paraeducator, your role may be to monitor while the teacher conducts these reviews. Another appropriate role for a paraeducator would be to monitor student understanding during the activities which the paraeducator has conducted.

√ Plan for reviews at the end of every activity that you conduct, asking yourself *How will I know that the students have learned the concept /material? What will they do to show this?*

√ Use any spare time you have with your students to conduct quick reviews of work. If students have finished their assigned work before the end of the session, use the time to give an oral quiz, have them ask each other questions or generate facts on a particular topic. It not only reviews the work but shows students the importance of not wasting time.

√ When you have extra copies of worksheets or other paperwork assignments, keep them to use as reviews. You may want to let students choose which ones to complete: they will be encouraged by having something familiar, and being allowed a choice.

√ Write items for review on index cards, and keep adding to them. You will then have a "bank" of items from which you can select 10 or 20 each time you review the work with your students. You should also have items that vary in difficulty as teaching sessions build on each other. Pairs or small groups of students can be allowed to use the cards as an extension activity when they have finished an assignment ahead of the rest of the class.

√ Bring games or flash cards for review of material or concepts that must be learned by rote or drill. It makes the students more excited and eager to try. If you have more than one set of flash cards, students can practice on them in pairs or small groups, and you can offer them as incentive for students to complete their work quickly and carefully.

√ Use story problems as a means of reviewing and checking for student understanding of concepts you have taught, particularly in math. Story problems are a useful means of checking for depth of understanding, rather than just knowledge of facts, but they are generally more difficult, as students have to 'extract' the math from the story and determine which math operations are required to answer the question at the end of the story. An example of a math story can be found in the box.

Math story (adding 2-digit and 3-digit numbers)

Three friends are helping on a community project picking litter in the local park. They decide to make a competition of it and see who can pick up the most pieces of litter in 10 minutes. Jay picks up 105 pieces, Fran picks up 119 pieces, and Matt picks up 91. How many pieces of litter do they pick up altogether?

Note: This math story can easily be extended to check for understanding of more extensive skills, as more able students can also be asked to find the average number of pieces of litter picked up by the friends, the ratio of the friends' totals, etc.

√ Have students write a short summary of previously covered work. Young students could be asked to draw a picture of what they remember, and tell you about the picture so that you can assess how much they understand about the topic.

Setting goals for improvement in my work

Meeting Learner Needs

The area I'm going to focus on:

The suggestion I'm going to use:

Time in which I'm going to try this suggestion:

How will I check on my progress?

What I noticed when I used the suggestion:

How will I include my supervisor in this goal-setting process?

CHAPTER 4: BEING PART OF THE INSTRUCTIONAL TEAM

Establishing your role and the extent of your responsibilities

We have already talked about the importance of establishing positive relationships with the students you work with each day. The other important relationships that need to be developed and cultivated – because they will definitely have an impact on your work – are the relationships with the other adults you encounter in your work setting. Your first priority should be to establish a collegial relationship with your supervising teacher – especially if you do not work in the same physical space.

√ When you start working with a new class, ask your supervising teacher to explain your role to the students, so that they understand both the extent and the limits of your responsibilities and authority.

√ If you are not sure of a procedure or have insufficient information to answer a student's question, ask your supervising teacher to clarify the issue. If the students see that you too are learning and willing to ask for information it will help to create a learning community in the classroom.

√ Solicit help and opinions both from teachers and other paraeducators, as they will all have had a range of experiences you can benefit from.

√ Be teachable and open-minded enough to accept criticism. Look on it as professional development, and be sure to ask for advice on how to improve in the area that has been criticized.

√ You can encourage your co-workers to make suggestions for improvement, or ideas on how to carry out your assignments, by making sure you put at least some of those suggestions into practice or use some of the ideas and feed back to the person who first suggested them to you.

√ Remember the basic rules of courtesy - be respectful, don't interrupt the teacher unnecessarily, especially when she's teaching.

√ Talk to your supervising teacher about your ideas for supporting student learning, and make sure he or she approves before implementing your ideas.

Keeping an eye on your own practice

√ It may be helpful to record one or two of your teaching sessions on audiotape. Although you may not like to listen to your own voice, listening to what you say gives you a chance to listen to yourself teach and to see what might need to be changed in the way you currently work. It will also give you a better idea of whether students have understood what you have taught. Audio-taping is often more useful than video when you are assessing your own teaching because you will not be distracted by visuals, and can concentrate on what is being said.

Establishing positive relationships with supervisors

In accordance with legislation, and for purely practical purposes, you must work under the direction of a professional educator. The extent to which you actually work together in the same physical space may vary, as will the level of supervision you receive for your work, but nevertheless there is a named professional who is ultimately responsible for the work you do on his or her behalf. This may be a class teacher, a special educator, a program director, or a school building administrator. Whatever the role of your supervisor, it is important that you develop a positive working relationship, so that you can exchange information on students, coordinate your efforts, and present a consistent approach to your work with students. A positive working relationship will also help ensure that you receive appropriate levels of support for the work you do. Consider these suggestions for ways in which you can promote and enhance positive working relationships with your supervisor.

√ Show your support of the teacher or other adults who work with you, especially in the presence of students. Make a point of dealing with problems (if there are any between you and another adult) in private.

√ Make sure you know what your supervising teacher expects of you and of the students so that you can provide consistent feedback and support for other adults and for the students.

√ Be aware of the strengths and preferences of the people you work with. Some people prefer to have things written down. Even if they don't state this as a preference, you may find they don't remember as well if you don't write things down for them. Others need to have things explained several times. This applies to adults and students, so adjust accordingly.

√ Be honest with other adults you work with. If you don't understand or know the answer to a question, say so.

√ If you don't agree with something and you feel it is not in the students' best interest, then appropriately express your concern. You bring another perspective which can be helpful, and need to get used to considering the perspectives of others alongside your own.

√ Be supportive of other paraeducators you work with, especially in front of the students. This is professional behavior. Speak to the person first, in an appropriate manner, if you want to take issue with something they have said or done.

√ Be sure that you have a clear idea of what you wish to accomplish, before you share ideas and ask for suggestions from the other adults. Keep an open mind, as their suggestions may warrant changes to your original plans.

√ If a colleague asks you to provide feedback on their teaching and interactions with students, be aware of the language you use and keep your comments impersonal. For example, when providing information on an activity and the apparent result, saying "When you asked the question that way, the students seemed to understand it best" is much less judgmental – and more helpful -- than "You were really good at asking questions"

√ If you want ideas, talk to your colleagues (teachers and paraeducators) about their work, what they are doing, and what they think is effective. There is a tendency to think that everyone does things in the same way, but we rarely know the details of what others do and we can benefit from their ideas--as they can benefit from ours.

Organizing for success

As a paraeducator, you are a member of the instructional team. You may not work in the same room as your supervising teacher, and you may not have much direct contact with him or her during your working day. However there are many things that you can do to enhance your relationship and to show you are willing to cooperate and to learn. Your supervising teacher has ultimate responsibility for what students learn and for what happens in the classroom, so it is important to establish clear lines of communication. Whether you are assigned planning time together or not, you can enhance the effectiveness of the team by keeping your teacher informed and showing your willingness to follow suggestions and learn from his or her experience. But you can also offer suggestions and changes to your supervisor without overstepping your responsibilities. Your experience in the classroom is also of value and you may notice things which the teacher, busily engaged in delivering instruction, may not.

Physical arrangements

√ Make sure students know the procedures and space for storing personal belongings. This may be a shelf or cupboard space.

√ Follow established routines for completed assignments: a tray for homework or a box for returned books near the door so that students can deposit their work upon entering the class; a file or in-tray for finished class assignments, artwork, or math books. Make sure students know these routines, and acknowledge them periodically for using them.

√ Reduce the possible anxiety and confusion for new students by explaining procedures and rules. Look at specifics: Do they need a hall pass to go out of the classroom? Do they need to raise their hand to get a drink of water? The other students can help to explain these procedures, and it will be a good review for them.

Planning

√ Ask your teacher if you can spend some time with him or her to plan the work that he or she wants you to do. Meet where it is private and where you will both be comfortable and uninterrupted.

√ Keep a folder of planning sheets that you fill out at the beginning of the term, and makes notes on them of what happens during the lessons, so that you have a system for keeping track of what you actually do, as well as strategies that work and those that don't. You then have a permanent and useful record of positive procedures that can be used with some confidence with subsequent groups.

√ Plan! Plan! Plan! Even if you are an experienced paraeducator, you should plan ahead for your assigned activities.

√ Spend time "brainstorming" with other adults those who work in the same classroom as you, but also adults from other classes or schools about what strategies they use for challenging situations. Be sure to keep names anonymous during these discussions, to maintain confidentiality. Experienced adults and novices can help you--the first because of their wide range of experience and the second because of the fresh perspective they are likely to bring to a situation.

√ Make sure you turn your cell phone off when you begin your working day – and leave it off until the end of your work.

√ Set a regular time each week for planning so that it becomes part of your schedule and one of your professional habits.

√ During seatwork, students need to know when and how they can ask for help. Make sure you establish these procedures so that they will know what is appropriate. For example, they will know whether they should raise their hand and wait for you to come to them, or whether they can approach you for help; whether they should go on with the next part of the task; what to do if this is the last part of the assignment and they have nothing they can continue with.

√ Don't plan on getting involved in other work, such as correcting papers, when you need to be circulating among students, checking for understanding or guiding practice.

√ The teacher may allow students to mark their own work, using answer keys to facilitate quick checking of worksheets. Even if it only saves you a few seconds per worksheet, you'll be surprised how much time it saves on a whole set. Students also often like to mark their own work, and certainly they like to have it marked quickly. They will also generally be honest in their marking.

√ Dig out notes and books from courses you've taken, to refresh your memory on skills you may have let lapse and effective practices you may have forgotten.

√ Use monitoring forms to facilitate record keeping, with separate forms for each content area. The forms can be set up for individual students or for a group, and should contain any information that will be useful to you, or that your teacher will need from you, such as scores, assignments completed, attendance. Keep the forms in an accessible place and fill them out daily.

√ Monitor student scores for your assigned groups, and share this information with the teacher, so he or she can make decisions about what you teach or have students practice.

√ Set aside a regular time to meet and plan. Situations change, so the planning which you do and the roles you assign at the beginning of the school year may need to be adapted to new student needs, changes in schedule, etc.

√ Where several people share a role or work together on a particular assignment, it is useful to keep a binder with papers and information relating to the assignment in a place which is accessible for everyone concerned.

√ If you work with students in more than one classroom, negotiate how you will communicate with the various teachers: how often, in what format, and for what purpose.

Confidentiality

This is one of the areas relating to a paraeducator's work that is most often addressed in training sessions because it is a legal requirement and pervades all aspects of your role. You represent the school or educational establishment where you work.

√ Do not share personal information about a student, including age, name, address, telephone, family circumstances, areas of disability or health status.

√ Information on a student's academic skills and progress or test results that you have acquired through your work should only be discussed with the teacher, or with the student's parent(s) at the direction of the teacher. You should not even discuss such information with another paraeducator who works with that student.

√ Do not share details of a student's social skills, particularly for those students following a formal behavior plan or modification program.

√ Keep information about other adults you work with confidential. Avoid gossiping or casually including personal information in conversations.

√ If someone asks you for personal details of an adult you work with, tell them you will pass the message that they want to get in touch and you will get back to them.

√ Pay close attention to the information you share, and adopt the practice of referring requests for information to your supervisor.

√ Keep written documentation out of sight. This might include student tests, IEPs, graded papers, health reports, disability reports, etc.

√ Enhance your reputation as a person who can be trusted by not giving out information inappropriately.

Setting goals for improvement in my work

Being Part of the Instructional Team

The area I'm going to focus on:

The suggestion I'm going to use:

Time in which I'm going to try this suggestion:

How will I check on my progress?

What I noticed when I used the suggestion:

How will I include my supervisor in this goal-setting process?

IN CONCLUSION

We have written this book in the expectation that it will provide you with a wealth of ideas for enhancing your work of supporting teaching and learning in the classroom, or other education setting where you work. We have also provided you with regular opportunities to reflect on how you can incorporate the ideas into your work – to try them out and check the results. We have addressed areas of responsibility which typically fall to paraeducators, who are assigned an amazing variety of roles. But we offer a friendly/final reminder once again that all of the work you undertake must be under the direction of a professional educator. We know what valuable contributions paraeducators can make to the education system. Take advantage of these apparently small but important suggestions so that you can continue to develop your knowledge and expertise, and thereby offer the best possible support for student success.

You may also be interested in recommending:

101 Ideas for Supervising Your Paraprofessional by Betty Y. Ashbaker and Jill Morgan.

http://a.co/65TtC8D

The Paraprofessional's Guide to Effective Behavioral Intervention by Betty Y. Ashbaker and Jill Morgan.

http://a.co/ce7mOCl

Useful websites

A websearch using your regular browser and the search terms *paraeducator* and *state* will offer you websites from the different States with a direct link to pages relating to paraeducators. These often relate to the different qualifications required of paraeducators in the respective States, but also link to training or professional development opportunities specifically for paraeducators.

In addition the following websites from a variety of professional organizations offer useful information and resources relating directly to paraeducator roles and responsibilities.

AFT. www.aft.org is the website of the American Federation of Teachers, one of the largest organizations for education professionals in the United States. Follow the link to *PSRP/School Support Staff* to find resources, news items of relevance to paraeducators, standards for paraeducators, and to download copies of the *PSRP Reporter* newsletter.

CEC. www.cec.sped.org is the website for the Council for Exceptional Children, the largest special education organization in the United States. Follow the link through *Professional Development* to *Professional Standards* and you will find the *Paraeducator Development Guidelines.* This is a newly revised set of Common Core Standards for paraeducators working in special education.

NEA. www.nea.org The National Education Association is another of the largest professional organizations for teachers and other education personnel. Under the *Our Members* tab, you'll find *Education Support Professionals* and a wide variety of information relating to paraeducators, including links to different State websites with news of paraeducators from around the United States.

NPR. www.nprinc.com The National Professional Resources website lists resources for educators on a wide range of topics, with pages specifically for paraeducators under the *Paraeducators* tab.

NRCP. www.nrcpara.org is the website of the National Resource Center for Paraeducators. There you will find links to resources, the annual Conference, news items and government legislation relating to paraeducators, as well as the chance to sign up for an e-newsletter and participate in online discussions.

In addition:

Check out www.amazon.com and use the search terms *paraeducator* and *paraprofessional* to find dozens of books for, and about paraeducators in the United States and Canada.

Look up www.continuumbooks.com and use the search term *teaching assistant* [this is the term used for school paraeducators in the United Kingdom] to find a whole series of paperback books written for paraeducators, on subjects such as literacy, numeracy, behavior, dyslexia, etc.

www2.ed.gov is the website of the US Department of Education. Using the search term *paraeducator* you can find a number of government documents relating to the employment and work of paraeducators as well as their role as part of the instructional team, working under the direction of a professional.

Bibliography

The following books have been written *for paraeducators* rather than teachers – that is, they address your responsibilities directly, rather than addressing the broader range of responsibilities which rightly belong to a professional educator. Some have been written and published outside of the United States. We include them here because they are generally available through online booksellers and because they address topics which may not be widely available in US publications for paraeducators.

Note: Titles by which paraeducators are known differ according to country. Items in this Bibliography which contain the term 'teaching assistant' all refer to classroom paraeducators.

Paraeducators in the Classroom: A Survival Guide
Betty Y. Ashbaker and Jill Morgan. 2012. Allyn & Bacon.

Developing as a Professional: A Guide for Contemporary Paraeducators
Mary D. Burbank. 2007. Wadsworth Publishing.

Teaching Assistant's Guide to Autistic Spectrum Disorders.
Ann Cartwright and Jill Morgan. 2008. Continuum Books.

Paraeducator's Handbook for Effective Support in Inclusive Classrooms.
Julie Causton-Theoharis. 2009. NPR Inc.

How To Be A Para Pro: A Comprehensive Training Manual for Paraeducators.
Diane Twachtman Cullen. 2000. NPR Inc.

Paraeducator's Guide to the Inclusive Classroom: Working as a Team. 3rd Edition.
Mary Beth Doyle. 2008. NPR Inc.

Paraeducators and Teachers Working Together
Susan Gingras Fitzell. 2010. Cogent Catalyst Publications

Paraeducator's Resource Guide [Reference Card]
Nancy K. French. 2008. NPR Inc.

Paraeducator's Essential Guide to Inclusive Education. Third Edition.
Peggy A. Hammeken. 2009. NPR Inc.

Behavior Support Strategies for Education Paraeducators.
Will Henson. 2008. [self published]

Portfolio Development for Paraeducators
Suzanne M. Koprowski and Carol A. Long. 2004. Allyn & Bacon.

RTI and the Paraeducator's Roles: Effective Teaming
Mary Lasater. 2009. NPR Inc.

How to be a Successful Teaching Assistant
Jill Morgan. 2007. Continuum Books.

Teaching Assistant's Guide to Managing Behaviour
Jill Morgan. 2007. Continuum Books.

CPSIA information can be obtained
at www.ICGtesting.com
Printed in the USA
LVHW051102181122
733432LV00009B/677

9 781539 706281